JUV/
PS

W9-ABQ-945

Historical American Biographies

PHILLIS WHEATLEY

Legendary African-American Poet

Cynthia Salisbury

Enslow Publishers, Inc.

40 Industrial Road
Box 398
Berkeley Heights, NJ 07922
USA

PO Box 38
Aldershot
Hants GU12 6BP
UK

http://www.enslow.com

Library of Congress Cataloging-in-Publication Data

Salisbury, Cynthia.
    Phillis Wheatley : legendary African-American poet / Cynthia Salisbury.
       p. cm. — (Historical American biographies)
    Includes bibliographical references (p.) and index.
    Summary: Follows the life of one of America's first black poets from her sale as a child slave on the Boston auction block to her death as an impoverished freedwoman in 1784.
    ISBN 0-7660-1394-4 (alk. paper)
    1. Wheatley, Phillis, 1753–1784—Juvenile literature. 2. Poets, American—18th century—Biography—Juvenile literature. 3. Women slaves—United States—Biography—Juvenile literature. 4. Afro-American women poets—Biography—Juvenile literature. [1. Wheatley, Phillis, 1753–1784. 2. Poets, American. 3. Slaves. 4. Afro-Americans—Biography. 5. Women—Biography.] I. Title. II. Series.

PS866.W5 Z694   2001
811'.1—dc21
[B]
                                  00-008882

Printed in the United States of America

10 9 8 7 6 5 4 3 2 1

To Our Readers: All Internet addresses in this book were active and appropriate at the time we went to press. Any comments or suggestions can be sent by e-mail to Comments@enslow.com or to the address on the back cover.

CONTENTS

This is the portrait that was included with Phillis Wheatley's book,
Poems on Various Subjects, Religious and Moral.

1

DEDICATION TO A COUNTESS

In May 1773, nineteen-year-old Phillis Wheatley boarded the sailing schooner *London Packet* in Boston Harbor. It was the exact place where only twelve years before she had arrived—a frightened, illiterate African child who had been kidnapped from her home and family by slave traders. This journey, however, would be different. Instead of traveling in the dark hold of a ship, chained with other slaves and sold to the highest bidder, Wheatley would travel as a first-class passenger. On her arrival in England she would be treated as a respected American writer.

Not long after she had mastered English, studied the Bible, and read the classics in their original

Latin, Phillis Wheatley began writing poems of her own. Realizing her special talents, Susanna Wheatley, her mistress, provided her with feather quills, ink, and paper. Phillis Wheatley would sit at a table and write poetic tributes by candlelight to Bostonians on important occasions in their lives. One of her first elegies, or poems of tribute (sometimes referred to as songs about death), was written in the fall of 1770. It expressed her grief over the death of the British Reverend George Whitefield:

> *We hear no more the music of thy tongue. . . .*
> *Unhappy we the setting sun deplore, So glorious*
> *once, but ah! it shines no more.*[1]

Phillis Wheatley had heard Whitefield preach many times at the Old South Meeting House in Boston, the church she attended with her owners, John and Susanna Wheatley. One of the most influential and popular evangelists of the Great Awakening religious movement, Whitefield's sermons often preached equality for all people. It was an important message for Phillis Wheatley, who had yet to gain freedom from slavery.

Phillis Wheatley's eloquent poem included an introduction written by Susanna Wheatley about the poem's author: "a Servant girl of 17 years of Age . . . but 9 years in this country from Africa."[2] Thanks to her mistress, Phillis Wheatley's poem appeared in a local Boston newspaper, *The Massachusetts Spy*.[3] Whitefield's elegy was later published in a pamphlet

The Great Awakening
Between 1720 and 1750, before the American colonies had won their freedom from Great Britain, a widespread interest in religion took place in America. This revival, called the Great Awakening, was an emotional movement. Its main purpose was to revive the interest of colonists in Christianity. The most famous minister of this intense revival was George Whitefield, who traveled from church to church and colony to colony preaching. Some historians believe Whitefield's words were responsible for Phillis Wheatley's baptism as a Christian.

read by audiences not only in the American colonies but also in England. It would turn out to be one of Phillis Wheatley's most important poems.

Behind the Scenes

Susanna Wheatley, knowing that the British-born Whitefield had served as the Countess of Huntingdon's chaplain, suggested that Phillis send the countess a copy of her poetic tribute to Whitefield. History is unclear whether this tribute prompted the countess to invite Phillis Wheatley to visit England or whether Susanna Wheatley arranged the whole trip.[4]

At the time, despite the success of Phillis Wheatley's pamphlet, Boston was not ready to accept a black female poet. Even women writers in more liberal England were using male pen names.

When Phillis's attempt to publish a book of poetry failed in the colonies, Susanna Wheatley became even more determined to get the poems printed. Wheatley biographer William H. Robinson wrote that Susanna Wheatley decided the poems might have a better chance of being published in London.[5] At the urging of Susanna Wheatley, on his next trip to London, Robert Calef, a sea captain, contacted Archibald Bell, a British printer, about Phillis's poetry. Bell agreed to publish the manuscript only if he had proof that a black slave had actually written such powerful words.

A tribute to Susanna Wheatley's persuasiveness was her ability to convince several prominent Bostonians to confirm not only Phillis Wheatley's identity but also her exceptional talent. Eighteen "respectable characters," including John Hancock (a future signer of the Declaration of Independence) and Thomas Hutchinson (the royal governor of the Massachusetts colony), questioned Phillis about her poetry and her general knowledge. Satisfied with her answers, all eighteen judges signed a letter, asserting that the poems in the manuscript had been "written by PHILLIS, a young Negro girl. . . ."[6]

John Hancock was one of the men who attested to Phillis Wheatley's identity and ability for her London publisher.

Only a Few Obstacles

Having decided to publish Phillis Wheatley's poems in England, Susanna Wheatley suggested renaming several poems to make them more appealing to British readers. Phillis Wheatley changed the names of several elegies. Titles such as "To Mrs. Leonard On the Death of her Husband" became more general—"To a Lady on the Death of Her Husband."

Phillis Wheatley's collection of poems would be published in 1773, just before the start of the American Revolution (colonial America's fight for independence from British rule). As a result, several pieces that might have been considered anti-British and pro-American were left out.[7]

A year before her book would be published in England, Phillis Wheatley composed twenty-three new poems to replace those poems left out. These pieces revealed a poet who had matured.

Before Captain Calef sailed back to England in November 1772, Susanna Wheatley presented him with a package. It included the preface to Phillis's book, a biographical sketch of the poet, a letter describing Phillis Wheatley's ability, and thirty-nine poems to deliver to the publisher.

Bookseller Archibald Bell personally read the entire collection to the Countess of Huntingdon. Impressed with Phillis Wheatley's writing, the countess told Bell she would be "fond of having the Book Dedicated to her."[8] Susanna and Phillis Wheatley

Not a Typical Slave's Life

Phillis Wheatley's education and treatment by her masters was unusual. The young slave had few household duties. She spent most of her time with Susanna Wheatley's daughter, Mary, who became her teacher. It did not take long for the family to realize that, "instead of obtaining a spirit born to serve, there had come among them a spirit born to create."[9] In colonial times, this opportunity for learning was an unusual achievement not just for a slave but for any woman. Phillis Wheatley quickly distinguished herself "as one of the most highly educated young women in Boston."[10]

were delighted. A dedication to a prominent person often increased a book's sales.

In a letter to Susanna Wheatley from London, dated January 5, 1773, Captain Calef wrote that the countess also wanted a picture of the young black poet to be included in the book. Believing that the picture would help book sales, Captain Calef offered to get an engraving of Phillis Wheatley done in England as soon as Susanna Wheatley had a painting of the poet completed.

Back in Boston, Susanna Wheatley hired an artist whom historians believe was Scipio Moorhead, a black slave belonging to the Reverend John Moorhead. This artist painted the only known likeness of the soon-to-be famous poet. Although there is no official record of the painter's name, Phillis Wheatley composed a poem that gives us a clue: "To S. M., a Young African Painter, on Seeing His Works."

Phillis Wheatley's portrait showed her sitting at a desk with a quill pen in hand. It was made into an engraving and appeared next to the title page of the poet's first published book, *Poems on Various Subjects, Religious and Moral.*

Doctor's Orders: An Ocean Voyage

Early in the spring of 1773, Phillis Wheatley was suffering from serious lung problems. Doctors said that the sea air might be good for her health.[11] Susanna Wheatley decided this would be a perfect opportunity for Phillis to visit England.

Even after Phillis sailed, Susanna Wheatley tried to keep the poet's name before the public in America and Great Britain. She promoted newspaper articles announcing Phillis's departure for England, referring to her as "the extraordinary Negro poet" or as "the ingenious [clever] Negro poet."[12]

On the next London-bound ship after Phillis's sailing, Susanna Wheatley mailed a copy of "A Farewel to America. To Mrs. S. W." to Phillis's publisher. It was a poem Phillis had written as good-bye to her mistress. Like most other important events in Phillis's life, her departure was recorded in a poem.[13]

The Sable Muse Is Crowned

Upon her arrival in England, Phillis Wheatley was treated as a celebrity. England had more liberal racial views than the American colonies. These liberal British views would eventually lead to the poet's manumission, or freedom from slavery.

The Countess of Huntingdon had arranged for the American poet to meet many important members of English society. Wheatley impressed the British nobility with her modesty and "powers as an incomparable conversationalist."[14] Phillis Wheatley took London by storm. According to historian G. Herbert Renfro, "Thoughtful people praised her; titled people dined her, and the press . . . 'celebrated' . . . the name of Phillis Wheatley. . . ."[15]

The English people showered Wheatley with presents. The Lord Mayor of London presented Phillis Wheatley with a rare edition of one of her favorite books, English writer John Milton's famous *Paradise Lost*. The Earl of Dartmouth gave her money to buy the complete works of another English writer, Alexander Pope, one of the young poet's role models.

Impressed with her abilities, London crowned Phillis Wheatley the "Sable Muse," or the black dreamer. During her stay in London, Phillis Wheatley also met famous American Benjamin Franklin, to whom she would dedicate her second book.

ADVERTISEMENT.

ALTHOUGH no poem better deserves to be printed with elegance and magnificence than MILTON's PARADISE LOST, yet there are so many splendid editions of this work, that it may seem proper to make some apology for the present.

It is printed as a companion to a late edition of HOMER; and, if the intention is favoured by the learned, VIRGIL may be executed in the same form.

This edition was occasioned by a conversation with Mr. CROSSE, Sheriff of this county, who persuaded the printers to publish proposals. These have been little seen beyond the walls of the University; yet, by his generous activity, and the frankness of the public, the subscriptions proposed were soon completed.

A few copies of the proposals were directed by the printers to persons of distinction, the honour of whose patronage and encouragement they had experienced on other occasions, and whose names are amongst the subscribers. That they are not more numerous, the printers must blame themselves.

Dr. NEWTON has taken so much successful pains, that though the printers were in possession of the three earliest editions, they never had reason to depart from his text.

This is a page from the copy of John Milton's Paradise Lost, *given to Phillis Wheatley as a gift by the Lord Mayor of London.*

Unfortunately, the poet had to leave England just a few weeks after arriving. Her mistress, Susanna, was ill. Phillis Wheatley had to return to Boston to take care of her. On July 26, 1773, the poet had to end her visit to London before most members of English society returned from their summer holidays.

Phillis Wheatley was not even able to meet the woman responsible for her triumphant stay. While vacationing in Wales, the Countess of Huntingdon had become ill. Although she had invited Phillis Wheatley to visit her, Phillis had to return home before the meeting could be arranged. Although she missed meeting some of the important people in London and some of the events arranged for her, Phillis Wheatley left England internationally acclaimed as one of the great poets of her time.

2

A NAMELESS CHILD IN A STRANGE LAND

To Be Sold
A parcel of likely Negroes, imported from Africa, cheap for cash, or short Credit; Enquire of John Avery, at his House. . . .[1]

One of John Avery's ads in the *Boston Evening Post* and the *Boston Gazette and Country Journal* probably caught the eye of John Wheatley, a wealthy Boston merchant and tailor, and his wife, Susanna. Most of the Wheatleys' household help was growing old. At fifty-two years of age, Susanna Wheatley was looking for a young black girl to take care of her in her old age.

John Avery ran advertisements offering slaves for sale for several weeks in the summer of 1761. As agent for the captains of Boston slave ships, Avery

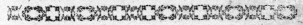

CHARLESTOWN, *April* 27, 1769.

TO BE SOLD,

On WEDNESDAY *the* Tenth Day *of* MAY *next*,

A CHOICE CARGO OF

Two Hundred & Fifty

NEGROES:

A RRIVED in the Ship

COUNTESS of SUSSEX, THOMAS DAVIES, Master, directly from GAMBIA, by

JOHN CHAPMAN, & Co.

⁎⁎ *THIS is the Veffel that had the Small-Pox on Board at the Time of her Arrival the 31st of March laft : Every neceffary Precaution hath fince been taken to cleanfe both Ship and Cargo thoroughly, fo that thofe who may be inclined to purchafe need not be under the leaft Apprehenfion of Danger from Infection.*

The NEGROES *are allowed to be the likelieft Parcel that have been imported this Seafon.*

An advertisement for slaves, similar to the one the Wheatleys probably read before they purchased Phillis.

was anxious to get rid of the cargo of the schooner *Phillis*. Many of its slaves were women and children, less desirable and profitable merchandise for slave merchants.

Timothy Fitch, the slave merchant who owned the *Phillis*, had expressed his concern about the quality of the shipment that Captain Peter Gwinn had brought from Africa. Gwinn had not filled Fitch's orders to avoid buying children, especially girls.[2] Avery was anxious to sell the human cargo or trade for more profitable men and boys.[3]

Susanna Wheatley Buys a Companion

Arriving at the Beach Street wharf, a niece of the Wheatleys told how her aunt Susanna went aboard Captain Gwinn's ship to inspect the slaves advertised in the Boston newspaper as "living freight." Among the cargo she found a small, sickly child.[4] Even with a dirty piece of carpet as the girl's only clothing, Mrs. Wheatley saw something special in the nameless child—an "intelligent face, modest demeanor and gentle appearance. . . ."[5]

Most biographers agree that the Wheatleys' newest purchase had been kidnapped from her family in the Senegambia area on the west coast of Africa. Little is known about Susanna Wheatley's new companion before she became a member of the Wheatley household. The only memory of Africa that the black child ever shared was of watching her

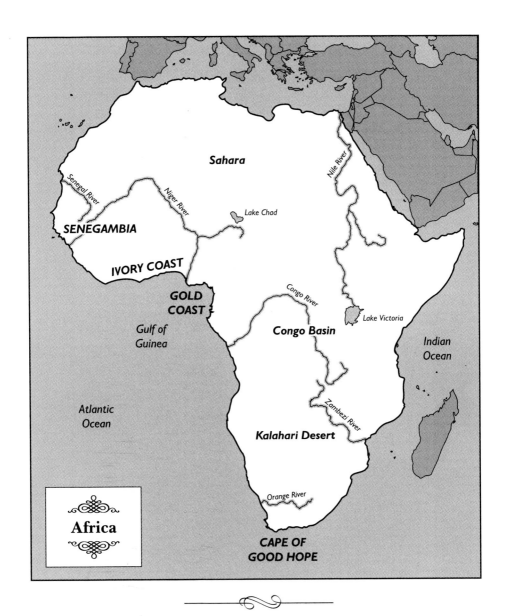

Phillis Wheatley was probably born in the Senegambia area on the west coast of Africa, from which many native Africans were kidnapped and sold into slavery.

The Business of Slavery

By the end of the eighteenth century, more than a million black slaves had reached the thirteen British colonies in America.[6] Merchants considered slaves goods to be sold for profit. Those who shared in the profits often captured families, separating them and selling them to different traders or taking only the men. Slave merchants based their trading business on one guideline: how they could make the most money.

Typical Profit for a Slave Ship's
Four-month Round Trip Voyage

Income:
Sale of cargo (217 slaves) $77,469
Proceeds from vessel sold at auction $3,050
Total income: $80,519

Less expenses:
Vessel, fittings, cargo, wages $39,700
Net profit: $40,819[7]

mother pour water each morning before sunrise.[8] This ritual probably had its roots in Islam, one of the religions practiced in the area of Africa from which she was taken.

There are some clues about Susanna Wheatley's new companion. Her frail physical condition, which would continue throughout her life, was probably a result of her capture and voyage. If the child had been one of the first purchased for the *Phillis*'s slave cargo, she would have remained a prisoner, never leaving the ship as it sailed to other ports on the African coast, searching for enough slaves to fill Fitch's orders. And she would not have been free of the *Phillis* until eight months later, after the slave ship had sailed the four thousand miles across the Atlantic Ocean from Africa to Boston. The long confinement may have contributed to her chronic illness.

Life on a Slave Ship

The voyage to America aboard a slave ship was a living nightmare for native African slaves. Many suffocated from being "tight-packed," a method of doubling the number of bodies on a ship to increase its profit. In a "tight-packed" ship, the human cargo could not move at all during the voyage. Fortunately, the *Phillis* was "loose-packed," which meant that, instead of one hundred forty to one hundred sixty captives, Captain Gwinn's ship only had about seventy to eighty slaves. Susanna Wheatley's future companion might not have survived under "tight-packed" conditions. Disease and starvation took their toll on every slave ship's human cargo.

With difficult living conditions on slave ships, revolts by the black captives were common. Most slaves had no idea why they had been captured.

Slaves tight-packed in the hold of a ship.

Some had terrible fears about what would happen to them at the end of the voyage. Rather than worry about the unknown, many chose to starve themselves. The bodies of those who did not survive the voyage were thrown into the sea.

A Home Far Different From Africa

With Captain Gwinn's price paid in gold, the thin black child probably rode by carriage from the wharf to the Wheatley mansion on King Street, a few blocks away. The Wheatleys' new slave caught glimpses of the sophisticated city that would be her new home.

The wharf at Boston Harbor was often filled with French, Spanish, and British sailors in uniform. As "The Hub," or capital of New England trade, Boston's docks were usually piled high with cargo— timber, wooden crates filled with peas and cod, and pigs—to be loaded aboard ships bound for England. These same ships brought back exotic merchandise and everyday necessities for the American colonists.

In 1761, the streets of Boston were filled with distinguished colonists doing business or discussing the political situation of the American colonies in relation to the British. Men wore white-powdered wigs, waistcoats, and breeches that stretched to the knee. Women dressed in hoop-skirted dresses with layers and layers of petticoats and wore wigs piled high on their heads.

Boston's buildings were mostly frame and brick, some as high as three stories. The streets had shops of all kinds—bakers, butchers, grocers, candle-makers, and tailors like John Wheatley. From these shops, the aroma of imported spices from exotic places such as China mixed with the colorful displays of fresh oranges, bananas, mangoes, and cherries from Madeira and the Azores.

Taverns served rum distilled from molasses and sugar from Barbados and Jamaica. The fragrance of brewing teas and coffees, imported from England, mixed with the savory smells of ham, baked beans, cornbread, and fresh peach pie being served to the

When Phillis Wheatley arrived, Boston was a bustling merchant town.

patrons of Boston's inns. Added to the potpourri of food and drink was the fishing fleet's daily catch of lobster, crab, cod, and shark. More than two hundred kinds of fish were pulled from the waters of New England during the 1700s.

There were some dark sides of life that even the "Hub of New England" could not erase. The Wheatleys' carriage probably passed some homes and businesses draped with red flags, signaling that they had been infected with smallpox, a reminder that Susanna Wheatley's sickly slave had not left the threat of illness behind.

Slaves: North and South

The North's economy was based mostly on small, independent farming and on trade. If slaves did not find work as deck hands or cooks on ships, there was not much for them to do except work as servants in New England households. African Americans represented no more than 2 percent of New England's population in the mid-1700s. Some Northern slaves enjoyed the same rights and privileges as freemen.

On the other hand, with an economy based on cash crop agriculture sold for profit, Southerners needed large numbers of slaves to produce crops such as cotton and tobacco. The South also had more laws controlling its "inferior" work force.

King Street and the Wheatley Mansion

Phillis Wheatley's new home was on the corner of King Street and Mackerel Lane. Susanna Wheatley's newest slave would live on one of the busiest avenues in Boston. With its chestnut trees, green yards, and sprawling houses, King Street must have been a startling contrast to the dark hold of the slave ship that had been home to the young black girl for months.

Neither slave nor master could know what lay ahead. Prosperous Boston, with its fortunes made from shipping and smuggling, would soon change as tensions grew between America and Great Britain.

3

A NEW NAME, A NEW FAMILY

When the young black slave stepped through the front door of the Wheatley mansion, her life would change drastically. Her new mistress, Susanna Wheatley, would play an important part in her life. Mrs. Wheatley's personal companion was given a first name, Phillis, after the ship she arrived on. She took the last name of Wheatley from the couple who had purchased her.

When she joined her new household, Phillis Wheatley became part of a family. Besides her fifty-nine-year-old master, John Wheatley, and her fifty-two-year-old mistress, Susanna Wheatley, there were two children—eighteen-year-old twins Nathaniel and Mary. Susanna, John, and Sarah, the

Wheatleys' three other children, had died at an early age. Besides the Wheatleys, the mansion on King Street also housed a staff of several aging black servants.

John Wheatley was a very successful Boston merchant and tailor. Distinguished colonists such as John Hancock were among his clients. His important business contacts would later be a big help for Phillis Wheatley. In addition to his businesses, John Wheatley owned one of the ships docked in Boston Harbor, several warehouses and some valuable pieces of property in the heart of the city. His store on King Street sold many items brought to America by his own schooner, the *London Packet*—casks of Lisbon wine, spermaceti candles (from the sperm whale), and crates of British tea.

Married in 1741, John and Susanna Wheatley were both deeply religious. Mrs. Wheatley is often described by historians as a "dedicated and sober Christian" woman.[1] Phillis quickly converted to the Christian beliefs of her masters.

A Slave in Name Only

John and Susanna Wheatley followed Puritanical views of ownership of another human being—"Slaves were regarded as persons and part of family. . . ."[2]

From the beginning, Phillis Wheatley was treated differently from the other slaves in the Wheatley

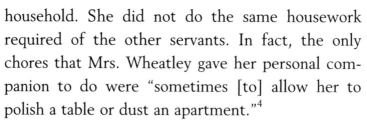

Phillis Wheatley's Neighbors: Puritans and Profiteers
Living on a hill overlooking Boston Harbor, Phillis Wheatley could see five hundred ships at anchor and eighty wharves, where schooners loaded and unloaded their cargoes. From a frontier town, Boston had grown into a city of eighteen thousand with sixty well-paved streets.

Looking more like members of the British upper class, the ladies of Boston wore lots of ruffles and hoop skirts, while the gentlemen wore powdered wigs, breeches, and knee socks. The Puritan ethic, however, was still alive in religion. A visitor to Boston from London observed that Sunday religious observances were stricter than he had ever seen: "Not just taverns, but shops closed their doors; no money exchanged hands . . . as soon as the sun went down on a Saturday's eve, Boston shut up tight."[3]

household. She did not do the same housework required of the other servants. In fact, the only chores that Mrs. Wheatley gave her personal companion to do were "sometimes [to] allow her to polish a table or dust an apartment."[4]

It may have been the observation of her quickness to learn that led to Phillis Wheatley's being home-schooled by Mary Wheatley, the Wheatleys' daughter. Unable to speak a word of English when she arrived in America, "within sixteen months . . . the

The Old South Meeting House, where Phillis Wheatley attended church, is seen here as it looks today. The building houses a copy of Phillis Wheatley's book of poetry.

youngest member of the Wheatley household was able to read . . . the most difficult parts of the Bible."[5] With Mary Wheatley as her teacher, Phillis not only mastered English but also learned Latin. Her daily lessons included "a little astronomy, some ancient and modern geography, a little ancient history, a fair knowledge of the Bible, and a thoroughly appreciative acquaintance with the most important Latin . . . works of Virgil and Ovid."[6] By the age of twelve, Phillis Wheatley was writing letters "on the most important and interesting topics of the day with many of the wisest and most learned in Boston and London."[7]

Phillis Wheatley's learning was an incredible accomplishment for a black slave. It was also an unusual achievement for any child growing up in the 1700s. Public education for most children in the New England colonies ended at eight years of age. And for girls, learning to read the Bible was considered all the education they needed except for learning "womanly things" such as housekeeping and fancy sewing. Girls from wealthy families sometimes went to finishing schools. Most private schools taught young ladies how to behave in society—stepping gracefully from a carriage or using the correct fork at a formal dinner party. Some finishing schools specialized in more "academic" subjects, such as music, painting, and drawing.

Circle of Friends

Phillis Wheatley had several privileges the Wheatleys' other servants did not enjoy—a room of her own, a light work load, and the opportunity to study. But Phillis Wheatley was not allowed to associate with the family's other servants. Most of Wheatley's biographers believe Susanna Wheatley tried to separate Phillis Wheatley from other blacks because she considered her personal companion more like a gifted daughter with exceptional talent and potential.

Biographers do not agree on how this isolation from her own race and culture affected young Phillis Wheatley. One story, however, shows how her mistress discouraged Phillis Wheatley's relationships with other black slaves in the Wheatley household: One day, while Phillis Wheatley was out on one of her many social visits, the weather suddenly turned cold and damp. Concerned that Phillis might get sick, Susanna Wheatley sent Prince, one of her black servants, to bring the frail girl home. On the carriage ride home, Phillis sat up on the driver's seat with Prince. When the two returned to the mansion, Susanna Wheatley reprimanded Prince, making it clear that Phillis Wheatley belonged inside the carriage, not outside, riding with the driver.

In 1766, five years after her arrival in America, twelve-year-old Phillis Wheatley finally became friends with another black woman. While vacationing with the Wheatleys in Newport, Rhode Island,

Phillis Wheatley met Obour Tanner, a fellow black slave who lived with a white family near the Wheatleys.

Because Susanna Wheatley discouraged Phillis's friendships with other black people, Obour Tanner was probably the only black person Phillis Wheatley knew well. Obour and Phillis had many things in common—both came to America about the same time, both were educated by their white owners, and both were deeply religious. Phillis Wheatley grew close to her new friend, often opening her letters to Obour Tanner with "My dear friend" or "Dear Sister."

"Your affectionate friend & humble serv't"
Besides her poetry, Phillis Wheatley left a collection of correspondence. These letters show a more personal view of the poet's career.

Wheatley wrote to a variety of people for many different purposes. With her friend Obour Tanner, she revealed personal feelings, including the philosophy of life the two educated black women shared. With a circle of influential correspondents in America and England, the poet asked for support in her writing career, including advice on business and religious matters. To the rich and famous, Phillis Wheatley often wrote letters to accompany the poems she had written about them.

Throughout Phillis Wheatley's life, the two communicated some of their innermost secrets. In her letters to Tanner, through which the two women developed a close relationship, Wheatley shared her joy in the common religious beliefs the two shared with other blacks, most of whom were slaves.[8]

Revolutionary Rumblings

In the late 1760s and early 1770s, colonial life in Boston began to focus on the treatment of the American colonies by the British government and the possibility of seeking independence from British rule. The seeds of rebellion were brewing outside Phillis Wheatley's window on King Street. Groups of concerned patriots, who were upset with Great Britain's taxation and harsh control of the American colonies, would soon turn to mobs and riots. And the newest member of the Wheatley household would have a clear view of what was to come.

4

PRAYERS, POLITICS, POETRY

Phillis Wheatley's new home placed her right in the middle of events leading up to the colonists' revolt against British rule. Boston would be the birthplace of the independence movement.

The Wheatley mansion was located in the middle of Boston's political, social, and business district, very close to the Old Colony House. Known today as the Old State House, it was home to Boston governors of the 1700s.

Boston, Center of the Colonies

With the third largest number of commercial sailing schooners "in the English-speaking world," Boston

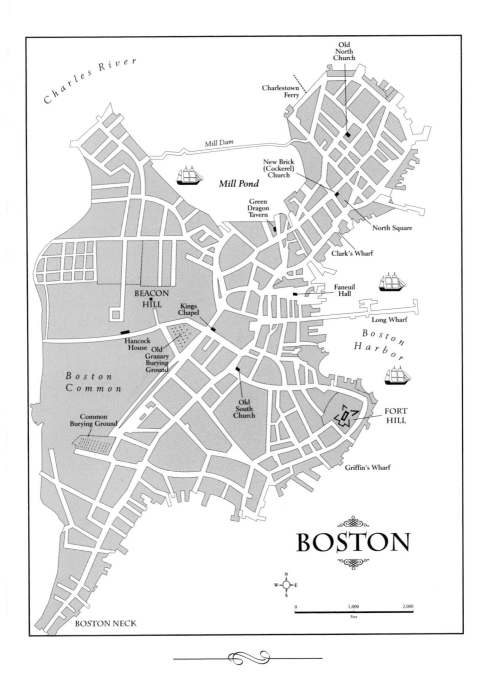

This map shows the city of Boston, as it looked during the years Phillis Wheatley lived there.

of the mid-1700s was the center of shipping and trading in the colonies. Suddenly, the town's shipping industry was under attack. British attempts to control American trade affected most of Boston's inhabitants by putting taxes on everything from sugar to paper documents such as newspapers and licenses. With these taxes and difficulties with overseas trade, Boston stood to lose as much as $164,000 in revenue a year and more than $100,000 in its shipping business, "—all for the sake of a motherland [Great Britain] few . . . [colonists] had ever seen."[1]

Taxation Without Representation

A secret organization soon formed to oppose British taxation. Made up of merchants, businessmen, lawyers, journalists, and others, the Sons of Liberty first protested the Stamp Act of 1765. This act represented "taxation without representation." Because the colonists had no representative in the British legislature, or Parliament, they felt Parliament had no right to tax them. At the heart of the patriots' fight for liberty was anger over being taxed without their consent.

The American colonists hated the Stamp Act. It required colonists to buy stamps to put on almost all important documents—even newspapers and playing cards. It also demanded payment for these stamps in "hard money" (silver and gold) rather than paper money. The colonists' paper money was valued at

King George III and the Taxing of America

Cheered by crowds in front of the Old State House on Christmas Day, 1760, the royal governor of Massachusetts, Thomas Hutchinson, announced a new king of England, George III. But Bostonians' positive feelings about their new king would soon end. In 1764, with the support of Prime Minister George Grenville, George III would start taxing the colonists to raise money Great Britain needed.

These taxes had devastating effects on Boston's shipping. Boston imported molasses and sugar from Barbados and Jamaica, made them into rum, and then shipped the rum to Africa, using it to buy slaves. The tax on sugar hurt Boston's trade.

When tea, one of the major staples of the American diet, was added to the British tax list, the American patriots' anger spilled over into Boston's streets with mob activity, revolts, and bloodshed. Not having access to reasonably priced tea caused anger toward the Crown—feelings that would soon lead the other New England colonies into a war for independence from Great Britain.

much less than British money. So paying for stamps often doubled what the American colonists owed the British in taxes.

With the Stamp Act came collectors to ensure that the taxes were paid by the colonists. Protests and riots became frequent. One August day in 1775, after marching in front of the Wheatley mansion, a mob of about five thousand protesters (about a third of Boston's population), demolished the building of the king's tax collector, Andrew Oliver. Oliver was supposed to begin collecting revenues from the newly passed Stamp Act. The mob's attack led Oliver to resign his position. This, however, was just the beginning. The Sons of Liberty would continue their protests against the British Crown's attempts to raise money by taxing the colonists.

Tea Brews Revolt

It was probably the colonists' reaction to an import tax on tea that tipped the scales toward revolution. The tea tax had been proposed by Charles Townshend, a member of the English Parliament. Known as Champagne Charlie, he had earned his nickname by giving speeches to the Parliament while drunk.[2] Townshend had been put in charge of British finance. When the British refused to remove tea from a long list of taxable items, the streets of Boston exploded in protest.

One of the most famous of pre-revolutionary protests against taxation without representation occurred on a street near the Wheatley mansion. A young student insulted a British officer. The soldier, who was guarding the customs house, hit the boy on the ear with the butt of his rifle. When the boy yelled out in pain, a small group gathered, soon growing to nearly four hundred men.

The angry crowd exploded against the armed British soldiers. The American patriots thought they were safe, because the British soldiers needed permission to fight back. According to historian Thomas Fleming, "someone in the unruly mob struck the soldier . . . knocking him to the ground. The man sprang to his feet and was struck by another club. . . . He leveled his musket and pulled the trigger." Seconds later, the other guards did the same. "The mob fled. As the gunsmoke cleared, Crispus Attucks [a leader of the mob] and four others lay dead or dying. Six more men were wounded."[3]

The Boston Massacre, as the incident came to be known, almost ended British rule of Boston. The Sons of Liberty outnumbered the British soldiers by five to one. Lieutenant Governor Thomas Hutchinson was able to prevent a bloodbath by arresting the customs guards and charging them with the murders of Attucks and the four others. John Adams, a future president of the United States, took the unpopular case of defending the British soldiers. John Adams proved that they had fired in self-defense. Even though the colonists lost the trial, the colonists' desire for independence from British rule was temporarily subdued.

A view of the Boston Massacre shows Crispus Attucks (center) being shot by British soldiers.

Beautiful Words About Bloodshed

Many of the Wheatleys' neighbors worked during the week on Boston's wharves. One of those men, Peter Faneuil, made huge profits in the 1700s—both legally and illegally. Many Boston residents smuggled goods to get around the taxes being imposed by Great Britain. Some patriots, such as Paul Revere and John Adams, were planning a revolution. Other colonists were busy making fortunes, an evil that worried the religious fathers of Boston.

While all this went on, young Phillis Wheatley did more than stare out her window. Having mastered the Bible, English, Latin, and history by the age of twelve, Phillis Wheatley had already begun to write poetry. Some of her poems reflected the events that led up to the colonists' war for independence from the British. Some showed her religious zeal as a converted Christian. Others commemorated the lives of Bostonians, telling of the births and deaths of friends and famous people who influenced the colonists fighting for America's independence.

One of Phillis Wheatley's verses described an event leading up to the American Revolution, which took place near her home. An eleven-year-old boy, Christopher Snider, was accidentally shot while on his way home from school by Ebenezer Richardson, a Tory, or British sympathizer. Christopher's funeral, one of the largest of the time, was attended by prominent Bostonians. Newspapers and broadsides, or posters, called Snider's killing a "slaughter."

In her poem "On the Death of Mr. Snider Murder'd by Richardson," the poet not only expressed what happened, but also made comments about who she believed was right and wrong. She described the scene, with the "young champion gasping on the ground."[4]

As the protests of Bostonians grew more extreme, the British sent troops to try to stop patriot activity in the city of Boston. In one of Phillis

Wheatley's earliest poems, "On the Arrival of the Ships of War, and the Landing of the Troops," she recorded the event. One of Wheatley's famous contemporaries, Paul Revere, also recorded the landing. Revere's engraving showed the British fleet anchored in Boston Harbor.[5]

During Boston's struggle for freedom from British rule, Phillis Wheatley made a direct plea for peace in one of her poems, addressed "To the KING's Most Excelent Majesty:" "Rule thou in peace, our father, and our lord!"[6] Although flattering, the words written in 1768 were not published until 1773.

Songs of Birth and Death

Besides the chaos and tragedy of the colonists' fight for freedom, Phillis Wheatley's early poems recorded other events that influenced her life. Shortly after her arrival in Boston, like the other members of her adopted family, she converted to Christianity. With the Wheatleys, she attended the Old South Congregational Church, a few blocks from their home on King Street. As a black slave, Phillis Wheatley could not sit with her family. She sat with other slaves in a separate area of the church.

In 1769, Phillis Wheatley wrote an elegy for Old South's minister of almost sixty years, Reverend Joseph Sewall. In Wheatley's poem "On the Death of the Rev. Dr. Sewell," the young poet painted a

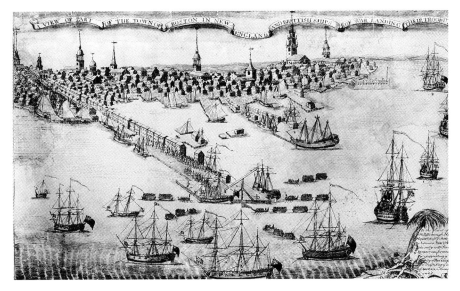

A view of the landing of British troops in Boston Harbor in 1768, drawn by patriot Paul Revere.

picture of Sewall, "holy man, arriv'd th' immortal shore."[7]

On August 18, 1771, Phillis Wheatley became a member of Old South. Because she was a black slave, the baptism ceremony took place after the regular church service was over. Her baptism marked the beginning of great changes in Phillis Wheatley's life.

5

FAME
WITHOUT
FORTUNE

Candles often burned late in Phillis Wheatley's room. Dipping goose-feather quills into an inkwell, she would write down her thoughts. With enough firewood to keep her room warm during the cold winters of Boston, the poet often worked late into the night. Her "untrustworthy memory . . . made it desirable for her to commit her ideas and poems to paper as quickly as possible."[1] Even though Susanna Wheatley often worried about the young poet's health as she worked late at night, Phillis Wheatley was always given enough parchment for writing and enough candles for light. Still, Phillis Wheatley's fame was not based on her writing abilities alone.

A Special Social Circle

In a time when many whites thought African Americans were not able to learn, Phillis Wheatley's unusual intellectual gifts put her on the invitation lists of Boston's elite and influential upper class, despite her slave status. Susanna Wheatley encouraged the young poet's growing fame. She often arranged visits from well-known ministers, merchants, and politicians to the Wheatley mansion. Many of these important visitors showed their appreciation and encouragement for the young poet by giving her books.[2] One volume, left by the Reverend Charles Chauncy, was an inscribed copy of Thomas Amory's *Daily Devotions.* Phillis Wheatley would later donate it to Thomas Wallcutt, one of the founders of the Massachusetts Historical Society.

The young poet's reputation as an intelligent conversationalist grew. Phillis Wheatley was invited to many Boston homes as the guest of honor for literary discussions. Thanks to the Wheatleys, the poet's social circle included influential politicians such as legislator John Hancock, Massachusetts Governor Thomas Hutchinson, and statesman and inventor Benjamin Franklin.

Phillis Wheatley was admired and sought out by many, in part because of her race and gender. A famous Boston doctor would later refer to the poet's intelligence and accomplishments as not only an "honour to her sex, but to human nature."[3]

One of the most often told stories by biographers and historians reflects Phillis Wheatley's position as a black slave in the American colonies. The story tells of an invitation Phillis received from the Fitch family. Invited for afternoon tea, the black slave found herself seated in the mansion of the owner of the *Phillis*, the ship that had brought her from Africa to America. Wheatley biographer William H. Robinson wrote that the Fitches' daughters were interested in Phillis Wheatley's stories, but were worried about the idea of having to sit down for a meal at the same table as a black person.[4] Some historians tell how Mrs. Fitch insisted that Phillis join them, and how her daughters soon were so charmed by the young poet's conversation that they "forgot her color."[5]

Color Lines in the Colonies

In the 1700s, blacks were not usually invited to socialize in the homes of white families. An invitation to be served at the same table as the white hosts was extremely unusual. Even Phillis Wheatley's exceptional talents did not eliminate most of Boston's racial prejudices. Margarette Matilda Oddell, a great-grandniece of Susanna Wheatley and one of the poet's biographers, recorded how Phillis Wheatley usually responded in these social situations: "Whenever she was invited to the houses of individuals of wealth and distinction, (which frequently happened), she always declined the seat offered her . . . requesting a side-table . . . apart from the rest of company."[6] Oddell suggested that this decision was not made because Phillis Wheatley felt unworthy to dine with the people who had invited her. Instead, it was her feelings about how her race was regarded by whites that kept her from joining them.

Whatever her place in these gatherings, Phillis Wheatley felt comfortable enough with her white hosts to take part in conversations about literature, the Bible, and other scholarly subjects. Through these gatherings, the young poet, who had perhaps a better education than most white Boston women, began to develop a reputation as a brilliant, young black woman.

Phillis Wheatley drew some social and political lines of her own that were not based on color. With the rumblings of the revolution increasing around her, she made some political decisions. Even though her poems and letters showed sympathy and friend-liness toward the patriots, she did not take sides and maintained many friendships in England and in America with those who remained loyal to the British Crown.

First Boston, Then the World

While her popularity as a guest in Boston's social circles continued, Phillis Wheatley was also seeing some of her poetry published. One of the first, dated

Poetic Themes, Words, and Titles

Phillis Wheatley's poems were influenced by her education, the events in her own life, and the people around her. Growing up in the Wheatley family, she was surrounded by dedicated, pious Christians. Practically all of her poems have religious references.

Phillis Wheatley also studied Greek mythology and read literature in Latin, including Homer's *Iliad* and *Odyssey*. Her poem "To Maecenas" has more than ten references to Latin poets, Greek gods, muses, and water nymphs.

Phillis Wheatley was also influenced by other poets, including Alexander Pope. She imitated Pope's poetic form, the "heroic couplet," a technique that repeats rhyming words and couplets.

She also used many grammatical devices in her writing—personifications (a figure of speech in which an idea, quality, or thing is represented as a person), alliteration (two or more words together that begin with the same sound), and similes (two unlike things that are compared using the word *like* or *as*).

Like most eighteenth-century writers, the poet used flowery language: "feathery race" for birds and "gentle zephyr" for a warm, pleasant breeze. Many editions of the poet's collections are footnoted to help today's reader understand her words, which may seem strange or old-fashioned.

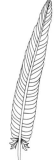

1765, was called "On Messrs. Hussey and Coffin." It was published on December 21, 1767, in the *Newport Mercury*.

The poem was based on a dinner conversation overheard by the young poet when Hussey and Coffin, friends from Nantucket, were dining with the Wheatleys. Her poem relates how the two men narrowly escaped from a storm on their way from Nantucket to Boston. While Wheatley's poem records the frightening event the two men endured, the poet also projected the worst for Hussey and Coffin, then placed them in the safe hands of her religious beliefs: "Suppose the groundless Gulph had snatch'd away Hussey and Coffin to the raging Sea; Where wou'd they go? . . . To Heaven their Souls with eager Raptures soar. . . ."[7]

A set of instructions, probably written by Susanna Wheatley, accompanied this poem and many others when they were sent to the printer:

> Please to insert the following Lines, composed by a Negro Girl (belonging to one Mr. Wheatley of Boston) . . . [Messrs Hussey and Coffin] . . . at Mr. Wheatley's, and, while at Dinner, told of their narrow Escape, this Negro Girl at the same Time 'tending Table, heard the Relation, from which she composed the . . . Verses.[8]

Unexpected Fame

Phillis Wheatley often visited her close friend and childhood tutor, Mary Wheatley, who married John

Lathrop in January 1771. Mary Wheatley Lathrop's husband was the minister of the Old North Church in Boston. Historian William H. Robinson believed that many of Lathrop's sermons inspired Wheatley's poetry about revolutionary events.

The real support for Phillis Wheatley's fame as a poet came when her elegy on the death of preacher George Whitefield was published along with Ebenezer Pemberton's *Heaven the Residence of the Saints*. The text of the sermon Pemberton preached about Whitefield's death first appeared on the same day that *The Massachusetts Spy* advertised Wheatley's broadside for sale. When Pemberton reprinted his tribute to Whitefield in Boston and London in 1771, he included Phillis Wheatley's elegy.

Wheatley's elegy for Whitefield would catch the eye of a very important lady in England—the Countess of Huntingdon. It would also help propel Phillis Wheatley to international fame.

6

LITERARY
AGENTS FOR THE
FIRST AFRICAN-
AMERICAN POET

The young poet, who had few chores assigned to her in the Wheatley household, could often ignore even these light housekeeping tasks when she felt inspired to write poetry.[1] More and more, she was treated as a member of the Wheatley family rather than as a slave.

Historian Julian D. Mason, Jr., wrote, "once Phillis began writing poetry . . . it was Susanna Wheatley who . . . encouraged her publication in every way she could . . . [finding] useful contacts [and] financial backing. . . ."[2] Mrs. Wheatley, acting as an agent, encouraged Phillis to distribute her works beyond the American colonies to influential people in England. She helped "publicize and distribute [the poet's] works through letters and in information . . . given to the newspapers and magazines," which often had not heard of Phillis Wheatley.[3]

When Phillis Wheatley's poetry finally reached the shores of England in 1770, Susanna Wheatley encouraged Phillis to write personal letters to several of the most wealthy and influential persons of English society: the Countess of Huntingdon; John Thornton, a millionaire and Christian philanthropist; and William Legge, the Earl of Dartmouth and King George III's secretary of state to North America. Susanna Wheatley, acting as a literary agent, tried to keep Phillis's name before the important people in London.

Attempts to Gather Subscribers

Firmly believing that she could get a collection of Phillis Wheatley's poems published, Susanna Wheatley asked Phillis to select twenty-eight poems that would be advertised as a manuscript in the *Boston Censor*. This list of poems would be part of a proposal to attract the necessary subscribers for printing the poet's first book. In the 1700s, publishers expected the author to contact a list of people who would buy the book when it was published. The money from the people on this list would guarantee that the printer could cover the costs of publishing the book. Susanna Wheatley needed

Publishing in the 1700s

Boston in the 1700s had ten printers, eight booksellers, six printer-booksellers, and several newspaper publishers. Most of these establishments were located near the Wheatley mansion on King Street. One of these, Cox and Berry, would eventually sell Phillis Wheatley's book.

For a writer to get something in print in the 1700s was not an easy task. Besides having to be able to pay for publishing expenses, writers or their friends usually paid for the advertisements for their books. A printer might put out a broadside or flyer at his own expense if he thought it might bring customers. Newspapers and magazines might take some financial risk and have a poetry section in the hope of gaining subscribers. But a bookseller wanted to know that his printing expenses would be covered before he went to press.

three hundred subscribers to secure the publication of Phillis Wheatley's first book.

Susanna Wheatley thought that getting Phillis's collection of poems published would be fairly easy. After all, some of Phillis Wheatley's poems already had an international reputation. In spite of the young poet's publishing credits and the Wheatleys' list of influential friends, attempts to gather subscribers failed.

It is possible that many colonists, especially those living in Boston, were too preoccupied with the effects of British rule on their economy to subscribe to or even to read a book of poetry. Even though most of the hated taxes placed on the colonies had been removed, except for the tax on tea, tensions between the British and the colonists still remained. Battles were brewing.

Boycotts on tea were being upheld in 75 percent of Boston's households. To show their disagreement with the tea tax, Bostonians were refusing to buy or drink tea, even though it was a favorite drink. The boycott had become "a point of honor. . . . Patriots served only coffee, tea smuggled from Holland or home-grown 'Liberty Tea.'"[4] The home brew was a poor imitation, often made from weeds. The boycott achieved its intended effect, leaving the London warehouses of the British East India Company crammed with molding tea.

A Change of Plans

Whatever the reason—the American colonists' pre-revolutionary concerns or their view of a slave as a poet—Phillis Wheatley's first attempt to publish in America attracted little response. Susanna Wheatley, however, had made up her mind that Phillis's poems could be published in London, and with this decision made, Susanna Wheatley acted quickly.

THIS DAY IS PUBLISHED,
Adorn'd with an elegant Eng·aving of the Author
[Price 3s. 4d. L. M. Bound]
P O E M S,
On various fubjects,——Religious and Moral.
By **PHILLIS WHEATLEY,**
A Negro Girl.
Sold by Mefs'rs COX & BERRY,
At their Store in King-Street, Bofton.
N. B. The Subfcribers are requefted to apply for
their Copies.

This advertisement tried to encourage subscribers for Phillis Wheatley's book of poems.

It was only a few months after her attempts to gather American subscribers failed that Susanna Wheatley asked Captain Robert Calef to bring Phillis's poems to Archibald Bell. When Bell understood the project and who its author was, he insisted on proof that a black girl had written it.[5]

A Distinguished Group Convenes

By October 8, 1772, a group of influential Bostonians had provided a statement for Archibald Bell, assuring him that a black slave girl had produced the impressive collection of poems. The declaration appeared in the preface of the London edition of

Phillis Wheatley's *Poems on Various Subjects, Religious and Moral* printed by Archibald Bell.

An Important Visitor

The letter of the eighteen "judges" was followed by a visit from a distinguished British representative to the Wheatley mansion, on behalf of William Legge, the Earl of Dartmouth. Thomas Wooldridge was sent to see the "very extraordinary female Slave." The Earl of Dartmouth wanted proof that the poet he had been corresponding with was really who she said she was. On his visit to the Wheatley household, Wooldridge was amazed to find a black slave writing poetry. Wooldridge also discovered, "by conversing with the African, that she was no Impostor. . . . I was astonish'd, and could hardly believe my own Eyes, I was present while she wrote. . . ."[6]

A Chronic Problem Turns Fortunate

Always described as frail, Phillis Wheatley would suffer from poor health all her life. Sometimes diagnosed with tuberculosis or asthma, she required constant medical care. In a letter dated July 19, 1772, the poet shared the state of her health with her friend Obour Tanner: "I have been in a very poor state of health all the past winter and spring. . . . Let me be interested in your prayers that God would please to bless me . . . for my recovery. . . ."[7]

The poet's doctors and Susanna Wheatley were always looking for ways to improve the health of the sickly black poet. It was because of these health problems that one of the most important events in Phillis Wheatley's life—her groundbreaking journey to England to visit her British admirers—would finally happen.

7

FAME AND FREEDOM

As Phillis Wheatley stepped onto the Boston dock in May 1773 to board the *London Packet* for her visit to England, she must have had flashbacks of her arrival in Boston on a slave ship from Africa twelve years earlier. But this trip to London would be a far different experience. Ahead of the poet was a social calendar unheard of for a black slave. Phillis Wheatley's days in England were filled with social events, gifts from important British people, and meetings with prominent American colonists and British royalty.

The poet's trip ended suddenly when she received an urgent letter from her mistress, Susanna Wheatley, who was seriously ill. On July 17, 1773, the poet sadly declined the Countess of Huntingdon's invitation to visit her estate in South Wales.[1]

Only six weeks after her arrival, Phillis Wheatley left London on July 26, 1773. The poet would never meet the "Ladiship" to whom her book of poetry was dedicated. She did not even have any copies of her first book of poetry, the only volume of her work that would be published during her lifetime.

Archibald Bell acted as more than a publisher. He wrote many articles about the book, some of which were outstanding sales pitches for Phillis Wheatley's book of poetry. In his September 13, 1773, article for the *London Morning Post and Daily Advertiser*, he wrote several flattering paragraphs about the author and her collection of poetry: "The Book . . . displays perhaps one of the greatest instances of pure, unassisted genius that the world has ever produced. . . ."[2]

With Fame Comes Freedom

While Phillis Wheatley was busy back in Boston waiting on her mistress, her book was finally published in London. Several English and Scottish newspapers and magazines reviewed the book. Unexpectedly, the reviewers criticized slavery, lamenting, "the hypocrisy of those Bostonians, including Mr. and Mrs. Wheatley, who loudly touted the talented slave poet, but did nothing to free her. . . ."[3]

Perhaps it was planned, or maybe forced by the criticism of the British reviewers, but Phillis Wheatley was given her freedom by her master, John Wheatley, shortly after she returned to Boston from London. In a letter to her friend Colonel David Wooster, written on October 18, 1773, the poet shared the news that, after her return to America, the Wheatleys had granted her freedom.[4] Even after the legal documents were signed, giving Phillis her freedom, she continued to live with the Wheatleys and tend to her ill mistress.

With Freedom Comes Responsibility

Phillis Wheatley also spent the fall of 1773 waiting for the first copies of *Poems on Various Subjects, Religious and Moral* to arrive from England. It was almost four months before the three hundred copies arrived. When her books finally arrived, the poet worked to find buyers for her collection throughout the New England colonies, even soliciting the help of friends.

Phillis Wheatley seemed to know that, with her freedom, came the responsibility of supporting herself. So she became her own agent. Notices advertising her book, *Poems on Various Subjects, Religious and Moral*, appeared in two local papers, the *Boston Gazette* and the *Boston Weekly News Letter*. Phillis Wheatley wrote to Obour Tanner, asking her friend to help her by gathering subscriptions

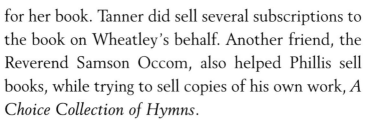

Susanna Wheatley

During the years that Susanna Wheatley had Phillis as her personal companion, she provided Phillis with an opportunity for an education. She also played a major role in her life by promoting her career and helping her meet influential people.

Susanna Wheatley kept Phillis Wheatley's name before the public in both Boston and London newspapers. Sometimes her promotion of "this girl, who is a servant to Mr. John Wheatley," as Susanna Wheatley referred to Phillis in the introductions she wrote, could be looked upon as "pushy." One example is the letter she wrote to a man who may never have heard of Phillis Wheatley.[5] She wrote the editor of the *London Chronicle* about the poet's departure from America for England in May 1773, saying, "You have no doubt heard of Phillis, the extraordinary negro girl. . . ."[6]

for her book. Tanner did sell several subscriptions to the book on Wheatley's behalf. Another friend, the Reverend Samson Occom, also helped Phillis sell books, while trying to sell copies of his own work, *A Choice Collection of Hymns.*

Phillis Wheatley's initial optimism about her mistress's recovery was short-lived. On March 3, 1774, Susanna Wheatley died at the age of sixty-five. She was buried beside three of her children.

Susanna Wheatley probably asked Phillis not to write an elegy because of her "Christian humility."[7] The only written record of the poet's grief is in a letter she wrote to Obour Tanner: "I have lately met with a great trial in the death of my mistress. . . . I was treated by her more like a child than her servant. . . ."[8] Susanna Wheatley's death caused a great sadness in Phillis's life. But there would soon be other events that would affect her life even more dramatically.

8

PAYING THE
PRICE OF
FREEDOM

I should not so soon have troubled you with the 2ᵈ letter but the mournful Occasion will sufficiently Apologize. It is the death of Mrs. Wheatley. She has been labouring under a languishing illness for many Months past and has at length took her flight hence to those blissful Regions, which not the light of any, but the sun of Righteousness.[1]

Phillis Wheatley wrote this letter on March 29, 1774, to British millionaire and philanthropist John Thornton. In it, she shared her grief over Susanna Wheatley's death. Thornton wrote back, volunteering to be Phillis Wheatley's "spiritual guide."[2] Because Thornton lived in England and she in America, Phillis Wheatley thanked him for his offer, but declined. At John Wheatley's invitation,

Phillis continued to live in the Wheatley mansion after her mistress's death.

Shortly before Susanna Wheatley's death, Phillis Wheatley wrote a letter to a friend not about the increasingly hostile American rebellion against British rule, but about the issue of slavery. In February 1774, Samson Occom, a Christian missionary and abolitionist, received the letter containing her feelings about freedom-loving Christians who owned slaves: "they preach True Liberty and how can such keep Negroes in slavery? . . . let them . . . set an example . . . by freeing their Negroes."[3] At Occom's urging, Phillis Wheatley's comments were printed in at least a dozen New England newspapers in March and April 1774.

The War for Independence Begins

On February 2, 1775, the British Parliament, upset over the violent rebellion that had now been brewing for several years, declared that Massachusetts was in rebellion. In April 1775, the British Army in America prepared to march to Lexington, a town near Boston, looking for hidden weapons. In the battle that ensued, ten colonists were wounded and eight killed. The British troops then marched to Concord to take the gunpowder the colonists had stored. There, three British soldiers were killed, along with two colonists. Before the British reached the safety of Boston, ninety-three patriots had been hit or killed. The British, however, suffered 273 casualties.

In June, only eight weeks after the colonists successfully responded to the British troops at Lexington and Concord, John Adams proposed a leader for the new Continental Army. George Washington was unanimously elected by patriots attending the Continental Congress—the new ruling body of the united colonies—to be Commander in Chief. The American Revolution had begun.

Life With British Soldiers

By July 1775, the fight for freedom had reached Boston. More than five thousand British soldiers were stationed in the city under the Quartering Act. This law was difficult for colonists to bear. Many Boston homes were occupied by both American families and British soldiers.

By the end of 1774, three British officers were staying with the Wheatleys. Two of the young men had served in Africa. Phillis Wheatley and the naval officers probably talked about their experiences in the poet's homeland. Three of Phillis Wheatley's poems, written during the months these officers lived in the mansion, reflect the influence of their conversations.

With so many British troops stationed in Boston, life changed. Without enough housing, defiant

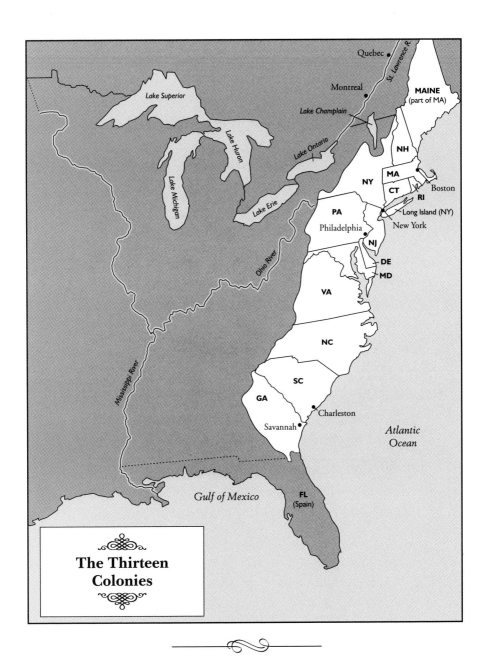

The Thirteen
Colonies

Quebec

Montreal

St. Lawrence R.

MAINE
(part of MA)

Lake Superior

Lake Champlain

Lake Huron

Lake Michigan

Lake Ontario

Lake Erie

NH

MA

NY

CT

RI

Boston

Ohio River

PA

Philadelphia

Long Island (NY)

New York

NJ

DE

MD

VA

Mississippi River

NC

SC

GA

Charleston

Savannah

Atlantic
Ocean

Gulf of Mexico

FL
(Spain)

*Phillis Wheatley observed the American colonies' fight for
independence from Great Britain from her home in Boston.*

colonists often left British soldiers to freeze without enough fuel for warmth, and without enough food to eat. Fights between drunken British soldiers, who were not happy to be on duty in America, and Boston citizens became daily events.

Soon, ten thousand people, of a total city population of sixteen thousand, asked permission from Governor Thomas Gage to leave Boston. With the port closed as punishment for rebellion, many laborers, sailors, and merchants were out of work. Families left Boston to find jobs in other towns. Others joined the militia fighting in the countryside. Some families left because they were Tories, who sided with England. They did not want to be forced to fight against the Crown.

According to historian William H. Robinson, "John Wheatley left town for Chelsea, across the bay. . . . Where the poet was during these years is uncertain."[9] Some pieces of poetry and a few letters Phillis Wheatley wrote in the fall of 1775 lead historians to conclude that she had probably fled to Mary Wheatley Lathrop's home in Providence, Rhode Island. Mary Lathrop was seriously ill. One of Phillis Wheatley's letters from Providence, addressed to a man who would be influential in the colonists' fight for freedom, would open a door to one of the most unexpected events in Phillis Wheatley's life.

9

AN UNFORTUNATE DECISION?

I Have Taken the freedom to address your Excellency in the enclosed poem and entreat your acceptance . . . the fame of your virtues, excite sensations not easy to suppress.[1]

Phillis Wheatley wrote these words to the Commander in Chief of the Continental Army, who was in charge of the colonists' fight for American independence from British rule. The letter, sent to George Washington at his headquarters in Cambridge, Massachusetts, included a poem of forty-two lines, which she had composed for him. Her words praised the newly appointed commander. "To His Excellency General Washington" ends with the following tribute:

Proceed, great chief, with virtue on thy side,
Thy ev'ry action let the goddess guide.
A crown, a mansion, and a throne that shine,
With gold unfading, WASHINGTON! be thine.[2]

Uncertain Years

During this time, historians believe Phillis Wheatley was living with her childhood tutor, Mary Wheatley Lathrop. When the British occupation of Boston began, Mary and her husband, Reverend John Lathrop, had left Boston to live in Providence, Rhode Island.

During the fall of 1775, Boston was occupied by more British troops than American colonists. These troops destroyed and scarred most of the city. Its mansions, including the Wheatleys', were occupied by drunken, bored British soldiers. The soldiers chopped down many of the area's trees for firewood.[3] The church where Phillis Wheatley had been baptized, Old South, was badly damaged. With the pews removed and used as firewood, the church was converted into a stable for the soldiers' horses.

An Unexpected Invitation

Four months after Phillis Wheatley sent her poem to George Washington, she received an unexpected invitation from the general. Preoccupied with the preparations for leading his troops into battle, Washington overlooked the poet's correspondence at first. On February 28, 1776, he finally read the poem. He then asked his secretary, Colonel Joseph Reed, to send Wheatley a letter thanking her and apologizing for not responding sooner.

Impressed with Phillis Wheatley's tribute, Washington extended her an invitation. When the general talked to his secretary, Colonel Joseph Reed, about the "poetical genius," it was obvious that George Washington had no knowledge of Phillis Wheatley's writing except for the poem she had written about him. In a memo Washington sent to Reed, he asked if he should address his letter to Miss or Mrs. Wheatley. Most whites of the time addressed blacks by their first name only. But the general, a slave owner himself, addressed his letter to "Miss Wheatley." It is possible that the general did not know that Phillis Wheatley was a former black slave. Most likely, he had not read any of her other works.

Only a few weeks after receiving General Washington's invitation, about the same time a bomb fired by American soldiers had badly damaged the Wheatley mansion in Boston, Phillis Wheatley was on her way to Cambridge to meet with General Washington.

Her visit with the Commander in Chief in March 1776 was remarkable. As a black woman, Phillis Wheatley was clearly not one of the typical visitors on Washington's busy calendar. Most of his

General George Washington, seen here sitting on a horse, invited Wheatley to meet him at his Cambridge headquarters.

appointments were with influential, wealthy people or with soldiers involved in the war effort.

There is no record of the conversation between the poet and the general. Wheatley and Washington met for about thirty minutes at the general's Cambridge headquarters. Shortly after she met with the general, Washington's secretary, Colonel Reed, sent Wheatley's letter and poem to the *Virginia Gazette*. Both were published on March 20, 1776.[4]

Revolutionary Changes

In December 1776, Phillis Wheatley returned to Boston. She was alone for the first time in the city where she had grown from an illiterate slave to a celebrated poet. Boston in 1776 was far different from the city she had known as part of the Wheatley family. The destruction of buildings was not the only change. When the fighting began, most of the Wheatleys' friends and supporters had fled the city to safety. Prices of housing, food, and clothing were three times more expensive. The war had damaged the Wheatley mansion. The poet had to find another place to live. For Phillis Wheatley, revolutionary Boston had become an unfriendly, inhospitable place.

Dark Days and Poor Choices

Through these difficult circumstances, Phillis Wheatley continued to write, mostly on patriotic themes. "On the Capture of General Lee" praised another American general, Charles Lee, who had been captured by the British:

> O *friend belov'd! may heaven its aid afford,*
> *And spread yon troops beneath thy conquering sword!*
> *Grant to America's united prayer*
> *A glorious conquest on the field of war!* . . .[5]

Unaware of what was happening behind the scenes of the war, Phillis Wheatley made a poor patriotic choice in General Lee. After not being chosen as Commander in Chief himself, Lee was jealous of Washington and disobeyed his orders. Worse yet, during his capture, General Lee drew up plans for the British on how to capture Washington's Continental Army.

When Phillis Wheatley completed her poem about General Lee, she sent it to the man to whom it was dedicated—James Bowdoin, a patriot and a future governor of Massachusetts. Bowdoin, aware of the conflict between Washington and Lee, chose to keep the poem private. It was not published until 1863, when one of Bowdoin's descendents found the manuscript. James Bowdoin's decision probably saved Phillis Wheatley from public embarrassment.

The Poet's Purse Empties

Now in her twenties, Phillis Wheatley could no longer support herself by writing. And she no longer had the luxury of being supported by a wealthy family or friends.

Those dark days for Phillis Wheatley were also shadowed by the death of her former master. On March 12, 1778, John Wheatley died. He left all of his estate to his son, Nathaniel, and daughter, Mary, who also died soon after. Phillis was not mentioned in his will.

Less than a month after John Wheatley's death, Phillis Wheatley accepted a marriage proposal from John Peters. The poet may have known her future husband for some time. Many Wheatley biographers believe that Peters delivered many of Phillis

Wheatley's letters for her. Historical records show that this was just one of Peters's many jobs.

A Questionable Choice

Referred to as "free Negroes," John Peters and Phillis Wheatley posted a notice on April 1, 1778, of their intent to marry. Friends and family had different opinions about Phillis Wheatley's choice for a husband. Obour Tanner, the poet's closest friend, believed: "Poor Phillis let herself down by marrying [John Peters]."[6]

Some of the Wheatleys also expressed concern. A few agreed that Peters had talent, but they described him as "too proud and too indolent [lazy] to apply himself to any occupation below his fancied dignity."[7]

Others had different views. Wheatley biographer Margarette Matilda Oddell described the poet's husband as "a respectable colored man . . . of handsome person . . . who kept a grocery store in Court Street, very handsome, well mannered, wore a wig, carried a cane, and 'quite acted out' the gentleman."[8]

Whatever his character, John Peters was educated. He claimed to practice law, and defended many of his fellow African Americans in court. Besides law, Peters dabbled in other careers—grocer, barber, doctor.

The one person who could have said more about John Peters was remarkably quiet. Phillis Wheatley

Peters never mentioned her marriage in any of her existing letters.

Dark Days Ahead

After her marriage, Phillis Wheatley Peters continued to express her feelings about slavery and freedom for all people through her poetry. She wrote elegies for friends who died in the war effort. Documenting the colonists' struggle for freedom, "Liberty and Peace, A Poem. By Phillis Peters," talked about the menace of "the Tyrant's Law," and the death and destruction of the war, and also gave a tribute to freedom.[9]

One of Phillis Wheatley's most personal poems was a prayer she wrote for her unborn child. Unfortunately, her prayer was not answered. Her first child died soon after it was born. This was the first of many personal tragedies that were to come.

10

CLOUDY YEARS

Soon after her marriage in April 1778, while her husband tried to find a job to pay the bills, Phillis Wheatley Peters tried to market her second collection of poems and letters. She could no longer rely on many of the people who had supported her writing earlier. By 1779, more than half of the eighteen men who had attested to her authorship of the first book of poetry were dead.

Not discouraged by war or death, the poet bravely tried to find enough subscribers to pay the publishing costs of another book by advertising in *Boston's Evening Post and General Advertiser*. Even with a dedication to her famous friend Benjamin

Phillis Wheatley first met Benjamin Franklin during her trip to London. He became one of her early supporters.

Franklin, and her reputation as a poet, however, Phillis Wheatley Peters's second collection of thirty-three poems and thirteen letters did not sell. Most colonists were still preoccupied with the fighting and destruction of the American Revolution. Money was scarce. Many of Phillis Wheatley's supporters no longer lived in Boston. And several of those who might have subscribed to the book were Tories. Many had left America. Without the support of the Wheatleys' money, a trip to England to try to secure a publisher was not possible.

The poet's audience had dwindled so much that her second book of poetry would not be printed in America during her lifetime. Although some of the poems and letters have been printed, the complete collection would never be published. Some manuscripts have never been found.

Ups and Downs of Married Life

In spite of this rejection, the poet's personal life seems to have been comfortable. The newly married Mr. and Mrs. Peters were living in a fashionable section of Boston. Based on tax records from 1780, the Peterses' home must have been one of the more expensive on Queen Street, where many important men such as John Quincy Adams and General William Howe lived. Each household had a staff of servants. Phillis's husband, John Peters, was listed in the records of the Massachusetts Historical Society as practicing law. Or perhaps, as William H. Robinson reported in his biography of the poet, Peters "kept a grocery store in Court Street . . . [which] . . . failed soon after marriage."[1] In letters to her friends, Phillis Wheatley revealed no signs of problems in her married life.

However, Phillis Wheatley Peters's personal struggles soon increased. When the attempt to publish her second book did not attract the necessary subscribers, the poet had to depend on her husband for support. And without the protection of the Wheatleys' wealth, the daily physical demands of caring for a house and family left the poet little time for her writing.

Shortly after her first child's death, Phillis Wheatley Peters became a mother once again. Motherhood was wearing on Phillis Wheatley's delicate health. When the poet had one of her many illnesses, there were no trips to the country or ocean voyages for rest and recuperation.

Moving to a New Home

Early in 1780, like many other Boston residents, the Peterses left the war-torn city. Historians do not know why they chose to move to Wilmington, Massachusetts. The small town north of Boston did not help solve any of the family's problems. Margarette Matilda Oddell described Wilmington as "an obscure country village [where] the necessaries

The Scars of War

In 1781, the British Army surrendered to General Washington's troops at Yorktown, Virginia. Although the war was, for the most part, over, the new United States could not yet celebrate. The Americans had won their freedom, but they faced the devastation of their homes, businesses, and towns. It would be a long time before Boston—where some of the war had been fought—would return to normal.

Food and wood were scarce. Anything that could be burned had been cut down or dismantled—fences, trees, wooden buildings. For decades after the war, mansions remained empty and in need of repair.

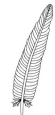

of life are always obtained with more difficulty. . . . Phillis suffered much. . . ."² While living in Wilmington, Phillis Wheatley Peters's health grew worse. John Peters's difficulty finding work in Wilmington and the birth of another child added to the family's worries.

Although there are no exact records of how long the Peterses lived in Wilmington, the best clue comes from Phillis Wheatley's letters and poetry. The poet wrote an elegy on the death of Reverend Samuel Cooper, dated January 1784, from Boston, so Mr. and Mrs. Peters probably lived in Wilmington for almost four years.

Back to Boston

Finding it difficult to support himself in Wilmington, John Peters decided to move his family back to Boston. Sometime in 1784, Phillis Wheatley Peters moved back to Boston without her husband. Why she made the move alone is unclear.

She moved into a house owned by a niece of Susanna Wheatley. Margarette Matilda Oddell described the niece as a "lady . . . a widow . . . not wealthy" who "kept a small day school, to increase her narrow income." Her mansion had been "injured" by the British, but it was a place where Phillis Wheatley Peters and her ill daughter were "ministered to . . . for six weeks."[3] (None of the names of Phillis Wheatley's children was recorded, possibly because each lived for just a short time.)

About a month later, John Peters joined his wife in Boston. He moved his family to a home far different from their former Queen Street house, where they had lived among the wealthy of Boston society. Historians described the area where the Peterses lived as a small, black ghetto in "an obscure part of [town]."[4] Shortly after moving into their home, the Peterses' second child died, possibly from some of the same health problems as her mother frequently suffered.

Soon after, some of Phillis Wheatley's worries about money temporarily disappeared. John Peters successfully applied for a license to sell liquor. He had procured a shop on Prince Street.

His shop, however, did not last long. Late in 1784, John Peters was put in jail because he owed money. In the seventeenth and eighteenth centuries, men who could not pay personal bills were often sent to debtors' prison. To pay off some of the debts he owed, John Peters sold his wife's valuable book collection, including her treasured copy of *Paradise Lost*, which had been presented to her by the Lord Mayor of London.

Once a Poet, Always a Poet

Fitting writing into her schedule became difficult with the demanding responsibilities of being a wife and mother. But even with the added hardships of poverty, Phillis Wheatley Peters found ways to write poetry.

In January 1784, the poet published a six-page pamphlet that contained her elegy for Reverend Samuel Cooper, one of the men who had confirmed that Phillis Wheatley was the author of *Poems on Various Subjects, Religious and Moral*.

Loss of friends, the destruction of Boston, the death of two of her children, and the poverty of her marriage made these difficult times. But the hardest times of Phillis Wheatley's life were still ahead.

11

A LIFE TOO SHORT

S everal versions of Phillis Wheatley Peters's final days have been written. Pieces of this period in Wheatley's life may never be known, because some of Phillis Wheatley's manuscripts and correspondence were lost, destroyed, or have disappeared into private collections. Some questions about the poet remain unanswered.

Writing During War

Most historians agree that Phillis Wheatley Peters's final years were spent "in . . . wretched poverty. . . . Living with the [her] third [child] 'sick unto death' . . . in a filthy apartment."[1] Her life had changed. Poverty and family life left her barely time enough to scrub floors and change diapers. The sickly, weak poet was performing all the chores required to keep a house and family.

John Peters could not seem to hold down a job long enough to keep his family out of debt. Phillis Wheatley lived her last days without her husband. Where he was is unclear. The best guess is that he was in debtors' prison.

During the last months of her life, Phillis Wheatley Peters and her third child moved to "a filthy apartment in an obscure part of metropolis."[2] According to historian William H. Robinson, "Wheatley work[ed] as a common maid in a boardinghouse for blacks in west Boston."[3]

In Her Own Words

Phillis Wheatley did not complain about her circumstances or her husband. Some attribute her silence to her intelligence, self-respect, and manners. Others point to the fact that women of that time did not usually talk or write about their personal situations. There is also the possibility that the poet's misery and poverty have been exaggerated by biographers and historians.

One of the clues that Margarette Matilda Oddell used to assert Phillis Wheatley's unhappiness during her married years was how the poet referred to herself in her letters. According to Oddell, even after her marriage to John Peters, the poet continued to sign her name "'Phillis Wheatley,' a name she sustained with dignity and honor. . . ."[4]

Letters written during the final year of Wheatley's life do not reflect any of the hardships of her poverty or the emotional pain from her two children's deaths. Phillis Wheatley's last poem, "To Mr. and Mrs. ——— [the name was unreadable on the original manuscript], On the Death of Their Infant Son," was typical of the other elegies she had written over her fifteen-year career as a poet. Nowhere did she share her grief over the death of her own two children, despite her personal knowledge of the topic. The only personal part of the elegy was a final appeal to the "Publick" for subscriptions to the poet's second book: "should this [work] gain approbation of the Publick sufficient encouragement be given, a Volume will be shortly Published by the Printers hereof, who receive subscriptions for said Work."[5]

A Death Unnoticed, A Grave Unmarked

Unfortunately, Phillis Wheatley Peters did not live to see her final works published. On a cold Sunday in December 1784, the first published African-American woman poet, who had been praised by a general and treated as a celebrity both in Boston and in England, died at age thirty-one without the comfort of friends, relatives, or even her husband. Historians list many possibilities that contributed to the poet's death—her chronic illnesses, the physical demands of being a wife and mother, and the birth of three children.

It is not clear whether John Peters attended his wife's funeral. He probably did not inform any of the few remaining relatives of the Wheatleys about Phillis's death and burial. A simple notice marking the poet's death appeared in the *Massachusetts Independent Chronicle and Universal Advertiser* on December 8, 1784, three days after she died. The announcement of the first African-American woman poet's death and the invitation to attend her funeral went unnoticed.

Final Words

"Liberty and Peace," written in the fall of 1784, was a poem of celebration. The four-page pamphlet, published after Phillis Wheatley Peters's death, rejoiced over the end of the colonists' struggle for freedom. The lines of the poem recalled many of the struggles of the American troops in winning the war—the costly Battle of Bunker Hill, where many British and American lives were lost, and the burning of Charlestown (a city near Boston) by the British. But "Liberty and Peace" also celebrated the ceremonies, sermons, songs, and parades held in Boston in honor of America's freedom from British rule—celebrations the poet may have attended.

Laſt Lord's day died, Mrs. PHILLIS PETERS, (formerly Phillis Wheatly) aged 31, known to the literary world by her celebrated miſcellaneous Poems. Her funeral is to be this afternoon, at 4 o'clock, from the houſe lately improved by Mr. Todd, nearly oppoſite Dr. Bulfinch's, at Weſt-Boſton, where her friends and acquaintance are deſired to attend.

This notice appeared in newspapers after Phillis Wheatley Peters's death, at the age of thirty or thirty-one (historians are unsure of her exact birthdate).

Phillis Wheatley Peters was buried in an unmarked grave, which may have been purposeful, holding with religious beliefs of the day that gravestones should be plain, so that only God would know who was buried beneath them. More likely, however, it was a result of the poverty in which Wheatley lived during her final days. There simply was no money for a fine funeral and gravestone.

Phillis Wheatley Peters was buried beside her third child, who had died a few hours after her mother. Because it was a cold December day, the poet was probably carried to the Old Granary Burial Grounds on Tremont Street rather than a dozen blocks away to Copp's Hill, where most of Boston's blacks of all classes were buried. With no friends and acquaintances to attend her funeral, Phillis Wheatley Peters's life ended in much the same way as it had started—in poverty and alone in a new country.

12

OPENING THE DOORS

With a career of less than twenty years, Phillis Wheatley left a rich legacy as the first African-American woman poet. She conquered enormous obstacles and became a writer in a time when neither women nor blacks were usually respected, educated, or free. Historian G. Herbert Renfro summed up Wheatley's contributions:

> She was greatly beloved and sincerely mourned by all who knew her. Superior by nature, impressing by her presence, charming by her conversation, exciting admiration by her talents, winning love by her tenderness, conquering prejudice by her Christianity, she commanded the hearts of the high and low, of the master and slave, and furnished the World another example of true greatness that would adorn the most cultured age.[1]

Lost and Found

When Phillis Wheatley Peters left Boston for Wilmington in 1784, she left her manuscripts in the care of Elizabeth Wallcutt, Susanna Wheatley's grandniece. Whether the poet retrieved her papers when she returned to Boston shortly before her death, is not clear. Nor is the reason Wheatley gave up one of her most irreplaceable treasures to the care of someone else. Perhaps the poet feared that her manuscripts might end up like some of her other personal possessions, sold by her husband when he needed money.

Shortly after being released from debtors' prison and barely two months after his wife's death, John Peters set out to retrieve his wife's collection of writing. Peters ran a notice in the February 10, 1785, edition of *Boston's Independent Chronicle and Universal Advertiser*, asking for the return of Phillis Wheatley's manuscript of poems from whoever had borrowed it. Peters said he intended to publish the poems.[2]

After collecting his wife's papers, John Peters did not publish her complete works as he had publicly declared. Near the end of the 1700s, John Peters moved south. He sold his wife's papers to Dr. Benjamin Rush of Philadelphia. Rush's wife, Julia, had been one of the poet's early supporters. If Peters had not sold his wife's manuscripts, many of Phillis Wheatley's poems may have been lost forever when John Peters disappeared several years after his wife's death.

Many of Phillis Wheatley's original manuscripts have been found. Others continue to surface from archives and private collections. However, five of the twenty-eight titles that would have been published if Wheatley had obtained enough subscribers for her second collection of poetry and letters are still missing.

Some of the unknown pieces of Wheatley's writing were her letters. Most of the letters that Wheatley wrote to British and American friends and received between 1766 to 1779 have never been recovered.

A Strong Spirit Lives on

Phillis Wheatley's legacy is not just what appears in her words. The poet's best gift is what all great people leave to those who follow—a belief in what can be. Phillis Wheatley's spirit lives on in those who overcome incredible odds to achieve, in those who rise above what is happening around them to record it for the future, and in those who set an example for others by leaving indelible footprints.

Much of Phillis Wheatley's legacy went unrecognized until several decades after her death, except for one incredible tribute written four years after she died. Jupiter Hammon, a fellow black poet still living as a slave, wrote a poem titled "An Address to

Miss Phillis Wheatley, Ethiopian Poetess, in Boston, who came from Africa at eight years of age . . .":

> Come, dear Phillis, be advised . . .
> While thousands muse with earthly toys; . . .
> Dear Phillis, seek for heaven's joys,
> Where we do hope to meet.[3]

Many blacks who might have read Wheatley's poems when she first wrote them were probably not allowed or able to read them. However, twenty years after the poet's death, when her first book was reprinted, Phillis Wheatley would have been delighted with the list of subscribers. Many African Americans bought the second edition of her *Poems on Various Subjects, Religious and Moral*.

The Mother of Black Literature in America

During the more than two hundred years since the publication of her first collection of poetry, many critiques of Phillis Wheatley's writing have expressed different views. Most agree that the body of work she produced in such a short time was incredible—one hundred poems, fifty of which were published by the time she was twenty.

Some critics suggest that Phillis Wheatley wrote on too limited a range of topics—religious themes, tributes to Bostonians, patriotism, and friendship. Her early words focused on what she knew and what was happening around her. Historian John Shields believed that Phillis Wheatley's many attempts to

Phillis Wheatley's autograph is seen here on a page of her book. In 1984, an autographed copy of her book sold for two thousand dollars.

record poetically the revolutionary events happening around her have been ignored.

The poet's correspondence to friends and acquaintances mentioned a wide variety of subjects, especially those Phillis Wheatley experienced: chronic illness, slavery, and abolition. But she also translated classic works from Latin and paraphrased biblical stories with great creativity.

Many historians have analyzed and discussed Wheatley's ability as a writer. Dr. Elizabeth James, a Wheatley scholar at Jackson State University, analyzed the literary value of the first black poet. She wrote that Wheatley's poetry was "a communication of her soul . . . a contemplation of what life was then, and of what it could be if circumstances were different. . . ."[4]

Recognition

Nearly fifty years after the poet's death, during the height of the abolition movement, Wheatley's beliefs and accomplishments became models for African Americans struggling for freedom from slavery. President Abraham Lincoln finally signed the Emancipation Proclamation in 1863, freeing slaves in the Confederacy (the South). A bloody civil war had to be fought to win freedom for all slaves.

In the summer of 1930, sixty-five years after the abolition movement ended with the Civil War, Phillis Wheatley received more national recognition.

A group of African Americans asked Phillis Wheatley organizations to make the third Sunday in February a day to honor the poet. The National Phillis Wheatley Foundation declared May 7 as a day to celebrate the poet. The date was the same day as the one in 1773 when Phillis Wheatley had sailed for England in an effort to get her book published.

The Abolition Movement

From 1830 to 1865, a movement to do away with slavery began by people called abolitionists. With the signing of the Declaration of Independence in 1776 came a belief in equality for all human beings. However, the belief did not become reality until after the Civil War.

The international slave trade (importing new slaves) was abolished in the United States in 1808. However, the South's economy depended on crops like cotton and tobacco, and slaves were a necessity to this economy. This was one of the main issues that eventually led to the Civil War, a war between the slaveholding, agricultural South and the increasingly industrial North.

American abolitionists never gave up. Their efforts influenced President Lincoln's signing of the 1863 Emancipation Proclamation. After the Civil War, the Thirteenth Amendment to the Constitution was ratified, finally abolishing slavery legally.

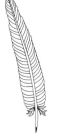

During the civil rights movement of the 1960s, Phillis Wheatley became popular again. African Americans, still struggling for equality, saw the poet as a role model. Phillis Wheatley was an educated, successful black writer who was considered "the Mother of Black Literature in North America."

No Gravestone, But Many Monuments

Since no one really knows where she was buried, a gravestone will probably never be placed for Phillis Wheatley. That fact, however, did not stop Boston, Massachusetts, from dedicating a monument to her memory. According to African-American writer Elizabeth James, there are "more YMCAs, schools, dormitories and libraries [named] for Phillis Wheatley than for any other black woman."[5]

In 1973, in celebration of the two-hundredth anniversary of the publication of the poet's first book, the state college in Jackson, Mississippi, held a poetry festival in Phillis Wheatley's honor. More than twenty poets and artists contributed to the festival. Two visual artists contributed by producing a painting and a bronze sculpture of the poet.

In 1985, nearly two hundred years after Phillis Wheatley's birth, the University of Massachusetts dedicated a building in her honor. Her portrait, based on the only known image of her—the 1773 etching probably done by Scipio Moorhead that appeared in her collection of poetry—hangs in

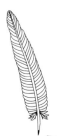

The Civil Rights Movement

Civil rights are the fundamental freedoms guaranteed by the United States Constitution—such as voting rights, equal protection under the law, and freedom from discrimination. The civil rights movement of the 1950s and 1960s tried to obtain equality and freedom for all black Americans by removing discrimination in housing, schools, voting, and employment. This struggle for equality climaxed with the passage of the Civil Rights Act of 1964 and the Voting Rights Act of 1965.

Wheatley Hall on the university campus. On February 1, 1985, the governor of Massachusetts proclaimed the day in honor of Phillis Wheatley.

As a slave and as a black woman, Phillis Wheatley represents an important symbol of the historic fight by African Americans for equality. Many books have been written about her life, her poetry, and her struggle for equality. Scholars still debate the meaning of Wheatley's poems. But her position as the first black woman poet was both a tribute to how she lived and how she accomplished what some must have seen as unachievable goals.

Phillis Wheatley's name appears in history books beside those who helped forge America's freedom from British rule—John Adams, John Hancock, Paul

This bronze sculpture, modeled after the engraving done for Wheatley's book, is one of the only existing images of the poet.

Revere, Benjamin Franklin, George Washington, and Patrick Henry. One recent social studies book described Wheatley as "the first important poet of African descent in North America. . . ."[6] This is quite an accomplishment for a person who arrived on the docks of Boston as a seven-year-old slave without a name.

CHRONOLOGY

c. **1754**—Born in Africa, probably in Senegambia.

c. **1761**—Taken from home and family by slavers to America on the slave ship *Phillis*.
Summer: Purchased on docks of Boston, Massachusetts, by Susanna Wheatley, wife of John Wheatley, a wealthy Boston merchant; The Wheatleys name their new slave Phillis.

1761 –1770—Learns to read and write from the Wheatleys' daughter, Mary; After learning English, Phillis also masters Latin and begins to write original poetry.

1768—British troops arrive in Boston Harbor to help control the colonists who are rebelling against British laws; Phillis Wheatley writes a poem commemorating the event.

1770—*October 2*: Phillis Wheatley's elegy "On the death of Reverend George Whitefield" is published in America; Her elegy is read by the Countess of Huntingdon, who will help get her book published in London.

1771—*August 18*: Wheatley is baptized.

1773—*May*: Phillis Wheatley sails for England, where her collection of poetry, *Poems on Various Subjects, Religious and Moral*, is scheduled to be published.
Fall: Wheatley returns from England; Shortly after her return to America, the Wheatleys grant her freedom from slavery, though she continues to live with the Wheatleys in Boston.

1774—Susanna Wheatley dies; Phillis Wheatley sends George Washington a poem she wrote in his honor.

1775—Washington sends Wheatley an invitation; The two meet at his headquarters in Cambridge, Massachusetts.

1778—John Wheatley dies; Mary Wheatley Lathrop dies; Phillis Wheatley marries John Peters.

1784—*December 12*: Phillis Wheatley dies in a Boston boardinghouse.

CHAPTER NOTES

Chapter 1. Dedication to a Countess

1. Phillis Wheatley, *Memoir and Poems of Phillis Wheatley, A Native African and a Slave*, 3rd ed. (Miami: Mnemosyne Publishing Co., 1969), p. 52.

2. Merle Richmond, *Phillis Wheatley* (New York: Chelsea House Publishers, 1988), p. 52.

3. Ann Allen Shockley, *Afro-American Women Writers 1746–1933* (Boston: G. K. Hall & Co., 1988), p. 18.

4. William H. Robinson, *Phillis Wheatley and Her Writings* (New York: Garland Publishing, Inc., 1984), p. 34.

5. Ibid., p. 28.

6. Ibid.

7. Ibid., p. 28.

8. Ibid.

9. G. Herbert Renfro, *Life and Works of Phillis Wheatley*, 3rd ed. (New York: Books for Libraries Press, 1970), p. 11.

10. Benjamin Griffith Brawley, *Negro in Literature and Art in the United States*, Rev. ed. (New York: AMS Press, 1971), pp. 17–18.

11. John Shields, *The Collected Works of Phillis Wheatley* (New York: Oxford University Press, 1998), p. 169.

12. William H. Robinson, *Phillis Wheatley: A Bio-bibliography* (Boston: G. K. Hall & Co., 1981), p. 18.

13. Shields, p. 120.

14. Julian D. Mason, Jr., *The Poems of Phillis Wheatley* (Chapel Hill: The University of North Carolina Press, 1966), pp. xiv, xv.

15. Renfro, p. 16.

Chapter 2. A Nameless Child in a Strange Land

1. William H. Robinson, *Phillis Wheatley in the Black American Beginnings* (Detroit: Broadside Press, 1975), p. 12.

2. William H. Robinson, *Phillis Wheatley and Her Writings* (New York: Garland Publishing, Inc., 1984), p. 4.

3. Ibid.

4. Ibid., p. 5.

5. Ibid., p. 6.

6. Richard Howard, *Black Cargo* (New York: G. P. Putnam's Sons, 1972), p. 30.

7. Captain Theophilus Conneau, *A Slaver's Log Book or 20 Years' Residence in Africa* (Englewood Cliffs, N.J.: Prentice-Hall, Inc., 1976), p. v.

8. Merle Richmond, *Phillis Wheatley* (New York: Chelsea House Publishers, 1988), p. 24.

Chapter 3. A New Name, A New Family

1. Jeffrey O. Krasner, Gerald Peary, John F. Persinos, Lisa M. Poniatowski, Alexandra Todd, Nancy Zerbey, *Boston in a Class by Itself* (Northridge, Calif.: Windsor Publications, Inc., 1988), p. 13.

2. Ibid., p. 12.

3. Ibid., p. 24.

4. Margarette Matilda Oddell, *Memoir and Poems of Phillis Wheatley* (Boston: George W. Light, 1834), p. 35.

5. Benjamin Brawley, *The Negro in Literature and Art in the United States* (New York: AMS Press, 1971), p. 16.

6. Ibid.

7. G. Herbert Renfro, *The Life and Works of Phillis Wheatley*, 3rd ed. (New York: Books for Libraries Press, 1970), p. 11.

8. John Shields, *The Collected Works of Phillis Wheatley* (New York: Oxford University Press, 1988), pp. 164, 165.

Chapter 4. Prayers, Politics, Poetry

1. Jeffrey O. Krasner, Gerald Peary, John F. Persinos, Lisa M. Poniatowski, Alexandra Todd, Nancy Zerbey, *Boston in a Class by Itself* (Northridge, Calif.: Windsor Publications, Inc., 1988), p. 28.

2. Thomas Fleming, *Liberty! The American Revolution* (New York: Viking, 1997), p. 50.

3. Ibid., p. 72.

4. John Shields, *The Collected Works of Phillis Wheatley* (New York: Oxford University Press, 1988), p. 137.

5. William H. Robinson, *Phillis Wheatley and Her Writings* (New York: Garland Publishing, Inc. 1984), pp. 16–17.

6. Shields, p. 17.

7. Ibid., p. 19.

Chapter 5. Fame Without Fortune

1. Julian D. Mason, Jr., ed., *The Poems of Phillis Wheatley*, 2nd ed. (Chapel Hill: The University of North Carolina Press, 1989), p. 5.

2. William H. Robinson, *Phillis Wheatley and Her Writings* (New York: Garland Publishing, Inc., 1984), p. 24.

3. Charles Johnson, Patricia Smith, and the WGBH Series Research, *Africans in America: America's Journey through Slavery* (New York: Harcourt Brace & Company, 1998), p. 144.

4. Robinson, p. 23.

5. Ibid.

6. Margarette Matilda Oddell, *Memoir and Poems of Phillis Wheatley, An African and a Slave* (Boston: Isaac Knapp, 1838), p. 15.

7. John Shields, *The Collected Works of Phillis Wheatley* (New York: Oxford University Press, 1988), p. 133.

8. Mason, p. 115.

Chapter 6. Literary Agents for the First African-American Poet

1. Margarette Matilda Oddell, *Memoir and Poems of Phillis Wheatley, An African and a Slave* (Boston: Isaac Knapp, 1838), pp. 18–19.

2. Julian D. Mason, Jr., ed., *The Poems of Phillis Wheatley*, 2nd ed. (Chapel Hill: The University of North Carolina Press, 1989), p. 5.

3. Ibid.

4. Jeffrey O. Krasner, Gerald Peary, John F. Persinos, Lisa M. Poniatowski, Alexandra Todd, Nancy Zerbey, *Boston in a Class by Itself* (Northridge, Calif.: Windsor Publications, Inc., 1988), p. 31.

5. William H. Robinson, *Phillis Wheatley and Her Writings* (New York: Garland Publishing, Inc., 1984), p. 28.

6. Elizabeth S. James, *Count All Black Voices* (Jackson, Miss.: Nekesa Publications, 1999), p. 23.

7. John Shields, *The Collected Works of Phillis Wheatley* (New York: Oxford University Press, 1998), p. 165.

Chapter 7. Fame and Freedom

1. John Shields, *The Collected Works of Phillis Wheatley* (New York: Oxford University Press, 1988), p. 168.

2. William H. Robinson, *Phillis Wheatley and Her Writings* (New York: Garland Publishing, Inc., 1984), p. 39.

3. Ibid.

4. Shields, p. 170.

5. Robinson, p. 34.

6. Ibid.

7. Ibid., p. 45.

8. Shields, p. 177.

Chapter 8. Paying the Price of Freedom

1. William H. Robinson, *Phillis Wheatley and Her Writings* (New York: Garland Publishing, Inc., 1984), p. 334.

2. Ibid., p. 45.

3. Ibid., p. 332.

4. Ibid., p. 50.

Chapter 9. An Unfortunate Decision?

1. John Shields, *The Collected Works of Phillis Wheatley* (New York: Oxford University Press, 1988), p. 185.

2. Ibid., p. 146.

3. Ibid., p. 51.

4. Ibid., p. 305.

5. Ibid., pp. 146–147.

6. Merle Richmond, *Phillis Wheatley* (New York: Chelsea House Publishers, 1988), p. 88.

7. Margarette Matilda Oddell, *Memoir and Poems of Phillis Wheatley, An African and a Slave* (Boston: Isaac Knapp, 1838), p. 24.

8. Ibid.

9. Shields, p. 156.

Chapter 10. Cloudy Years

1. William H. Robinson, *Phillis Wheatley in the Black American Beginnings* (Detroit: Broadside Press, 1975), p. 53.

2. Margarette Matilda Oddell, *Memoir and Poems of Phillis Wheatley, An African and a Slave* (Boston: Isaac Knapp, 1838), p. 25.

3. Ibid., p. 8.

4. Robinson, p. 58.

Chapter 11. A Life Too Short

1. William H. Robinson, *Phillis Wheatley in the Black American Beginnings* (Detroit: Broadside Press, 1975), p. 60.

2. Margarette Matilda Oddell, *Memoir and Poems of Phillis Wheatley, An African and a Slave* (Boston: Isaac Knapp, 1838), p. 28.

3. William Henry Robinson, *Phillis Wheatley* (Boston: The Old South Association, 1990), p. 15.

4. Oddell, p. 26.

5. Robinson, pp. 63–64.

Chapter 12. Opening the Doors

1. G. Herbert Renfro, *The Life and Works of Phillis Wheatley*, 3rd ed. (New York: Books for Libraries Press, 1970), p. 25.

2. William H. Robinson, *Phillis Wheatley and Her Writings* (New York: Garland Publishing, Inc., 1984), p. 65.

3. Sondra A. O'Neale, *Jupiter Hammon and the Biblical Beginnings of African-American Literature* (Lanham, Md.: The Scarecrow Press, Inc., 1993), pp. 74–75.

4. Elizabeth S. James, *Count All Black Voices* (Jackson, Miss.: Nekesa Publications, 1999), pp. 34–35.

5. Robinson, p. 69.

6. Beverly J. Armento, J. Jorge Klor de Avla, Gary B. Nash, Christopher L. Salter, Louis E. Wilson, and Karen K. Wixson, *America Will Be* (Boston: Houghton Mifflin Company, 1994), p. 235.

GLOSSARY

abolition—The legal end of slavery.

boycott—To stop buying something to force someone to do something.

elite—The best or most powerful of a group of people.

evangelist—A preacher or clergyman who traveled, reviving interest in religion.

merchant—A person who buys and sells goods for a profit.

metaphor—A word or group of words used to describe what another word is like, although not usually associated with the word being described.

musket—A large, heavy gun.

parchment—Paper made from goat or sheep skin.

philanthropist—A person who is interested in the welfare of fellow human beings and expresses concern by donating money or gifts.

pious—Devoted to religion.

Puritan—A person who follows a strict set of religious beliefs. Puritans were especially influential in the 1600s and 1700s in the American colonies.

quills—Writing pens made from the large feathers of a bird.

rebellion—Resistance to authority, often by means of armed demonstrations.

schooner—A large sailing ship with two or more main masts and fore and aft sails.

simile—A figure of speech that compares two unlike things using the word *like* or *as*.

Sons of Liberty—A group formed in Boston to protest British taxation of the American colonists.

FURTHER READING

Books

Fleming, Thomas. *Liberty! The American Revolution.* New York: Viking, 1997.

Hull, Mary E. *The Boston Tea Party in American History.* Springfield, N.J.: Enslow Publishers, Inc., 1999.

Kent, Deborah. *The American Revolution: "Give Me Liberty, or Give Me Death!"* Hillside, N.J.: Enslow Publishers, Inc., 1994.

Richmond, Merle. *Phillis Wheatley.* New York: Chelsea House Publishers, 1988.

Weidt, Maryann N. *Revolutionary Poet.* Minneapolis: Carolrhoda Books, Inc., 1997.

Internet Addresses

Bailey, Roger Blackwell. "The Phyllis Wheatley Page." *San Antonio College LitWeb*. n.d. <http://www.accd.edu/sac/english/bailey/wheatley.htm> (June 8, 2000).

The Massachusetts Historical Society. 2000. <http://masshist.org/> (June 8, 2000).

PBS Online. "Diversity and Phyllis Wheatley." *Liberty!* 1997. <http://www.pbs.org/ktca/liberty/chronicle/diversity-phyllisw.html> (June 8, 2000).

INDEX